Curriculum Visions

Sikh gurdwara

Stained glass window in a gurdwara

Lisa Magloff

Word list

Look out for these words as you go through the book. They are shown using CAPITALS.

5Ks Five symbols of Sikhism that all baptised Sikhs should wear at all times. The 5Ks are: kesh, khanga, kara, kaccha and kirpan.

AKHAND PATH A ceremony in which the entire Guru Granth Sahib is read out loud, nonstop. It takes about 48 hours, and different people take turns reading.

ARDAS One of the main Sikh congregational prayers, written during the 18th century.

BAPTISM The English word for when a person becomes a full member of a particular religious community.

CHAURI A fan made of yak hair or another fibre, placed in a wooden handle. The chauri is waved over the Guru Granth Sahib whenever it is being read, as a symbol of respect.

DARBAR The room in a gurdwara where group worship takes place. Also called a diwan hall. The Guru Granth Sahib is in the darbar during worship.

DIWAN A word meaning group worship.

GRANTHI The person who performs the reading of the Guru Granth Sahib at religious occasions; it may be a man or a woman. In a large gurdwara, the granthi may also have other responsibilities, such as putting the Guru Granth Sahib in its own room at night and taking it out in the morning.

GURDWARA The name given to a Sikh temple. It means "doorway to the house of God".

GURU A Sanskrit word meaning teacher, honoured person, religious person or saint. Sanskrit is a language spoken in ancient India.

GURU GRANTH SAHIB The holy book of Sikhism. It is also called the adi-granth. The word "adi" means the original, first. The Guru Granth contains the scriptures of Sikhism. It is regarded as the living body and voice of the gurus.

GURUPURAB The celebration of the anniversary of the birth or death of a guru.

KACCHA Drawers or briefs. One of the five physical symbols that a baptised Sikh must wear.

KARA Steel bracelet, one of the five physical symbols that a baptised Sikh must wear. It is a symbol of restraint and remembrance of God.

KARDH PARSHAD A food served at religious ceremonies in the presence of the Guru Granth Sahib and sanctified by prayers.

KESH Uncut hair, one of the five physical symbols that a baptised Sikh must have. It is a symbol of spirituality.

KHALSA A word meaning "pure". This is the name given by Guru Gobind Singh to all Sikhs who have been baptised in the Amrit ceremony. All members of the khalsa should carry the 5Ks.

KHANDA The emblem of the Sikh nation, named after the double edged sword in the middle.

KHANGA A small comb, one of the five physical symbols that a baptised Sikh must wear. It is normally worn in the hair and is a symbol of cleanliness, order and discipline.

KIRPAN A sword, one of the five physical symbols that a khalsa Sikh must wear. It is a symbol of the Sikh fight against injustice and religious oppression.

KIRTAN The singing of sacred hymns from the Guru Granth Sahib to music.

LANGAR A kitchen found in every gurdwara which serves free food to all people irrespective of their caste, creed, colour or status.

PALKI A canopy which covers the Guru Granth Sahib whenever it is on display or being read.

PANGAT A meal eaten in the langar after worship.

PUNJABI The language of the Punjab. Punjabi is also the word for a person from the Punjab.

RAGI A musician who plays traditional instruments as part of Sikh worship services.

SACHKAND A small room in a gurdwara where the Guru Granth Sahib is placed during the night.

SEWA The word sewa means service or voluntary, and stands for the importance of helping others.

SIKH A person who follows the teachings of Guru Nanak Dev and of the Guru Granth Sahib.

TAKHT A word meaning throne, or the seat of royal, temporal or spiritual authority. The takht is a platform where the Guru Granth Sahib is placed whenever it is in the darbar.

Contents

Be considerate!

When visiting a place of worship, remember that it is sacred to believers and so be considerate to their feelings. It doesn't take a lot of effort – just attitude.

Traditional Sikh clothing

What is a gurdwara?

A gurdwara is both a place where Sikhs go to worship together, and a centre for the Sikh community.

A **GURDWARA** is a place where **SIKHS** worship together (pictures ① and ②), just as Hindus worship together in a mandir and Christians in a church.

▼ ① A gurdwara can be large or small. This gurdwara in London is one of the largest in Europe.

▲ ② These people are entering the gurdwara for worship.

The word GURU means religious teacher. Sikhism was founded around 530 years ago by Guru Nanak Dev, a man who lived in the Punjab region of India and Pakistan. In the PUNJABI language, the word Sikh means religious student. So a Sikh is someone who follows the teachings of Guru Nanak Dev and the nine Sikh gurus who taught after him.

◀ (3) **Sometimes, the words "Ik onkar", meaning "God is one" are written on the outside of the gurdwara in Punjabi. These are the first words in the Guru Granth Sahib.**

The gurdwara

In Punjabi, the word gurdwara means "doorway to the house of God".

In Sikhism, prayers to God can be offered any time and any place, but worshipping with other people is very imporant, which is why many Sikhs go to a gurdwara every day.

The gurdwara is more than a place to pray. It is also a social centre for the Sikh community, a place where people can meet and where everyone is welcome.

The Sikh holy book

Guru Nanak Dev taught that there is one God who is all powerful (picture (3)), and that all people are equal, no matter what race, creed, belief or gender they are. He also taught that it is important to work hard, to help others and to always try to improve yourself.

The tenth, and last, Sikh guru died in 1708. Before he died, he collected all the sayings and writings of all the Sikh gurus into a book, called the Sri **GURU GRANTH SAHIB**. This is the holy book of Sikhism.

Punjabi traditions

Although there are Sikhs living all over the world, most Sikhs are Punjabi. So, many of the traditions and aspects of the Sikh religion come from the Punjabi culture.

For example, gurdwaras around the world are often built in the same style as gurdwaras in the Punjab. The Guru Granth Sahib is written in the Punjabi language, and most of the words used in Sikhism are in Punjabi.

When Sikhs share a meal after worship, they may eat traditional Punjabi food and many of the people you see inside the gurdwara are dressed in traditional Punjabi clothes.

A way of life

Sikhism is more than worship at the gurdwara, it is a way of life.

Sikhism is not only a set of beliefs, it is a way of acting and behaving all of the time. As a reminder of this, there are five important symbols of Sikhism that are worn by most adult Sikhs. These symbols are worn not only at the gurdwara, but all the time. They are a part of the Sikh way of life and of worship both inside and outside of the gurdwara. These symbols are visible reminders of Sikh beliefs.

Because the name of each symbol begins with a K, they are sometimes called the five Ks (**5Ks**). They are: **KESH** (uncut hair), **KHANGA** (wooden comb), **KARA** (steel bracelet), **KACCHA** (a type of underwear) and **KIRPAN** (sword).

Kesh, khanga and turban

Sikhs believe that uncut hair, called kesh, is a sign of living in harmony with God, so many Sikhs do not cut their hair. They wear a wooden comb, called a khanga (picture ③) as a reminder of how important it is to keep their long hair neat and clean. The turban (picture ②) also helps keep the long hair neat and out of the way. Instead of a turban, women keep their hair neat by wearing a scarf or a shawl.

Kara

When Sikhism began, many rich people in the Punjab wore expensive gold or silver bracelets. Sikhs wear a simple steel bracelet instead (picture ①). The circle of the bracelet is a reminder that God has no beginning or end, the steel is a reminder to always have the strength to make the right decisions, and the simple design is a reminder that all people are equal.

▶ ② A turban. This man also does not cut his beard or moustache.

▲ ① A simple silver kara.

▲ ③ Many Sikhs today find that it is not practical to wear large khanga and kirpan all the time. Instead, they may wear tiny kirpan and khanga around their necks. The third symbol here is a double edged sword, which is another symbol of Sikhism.

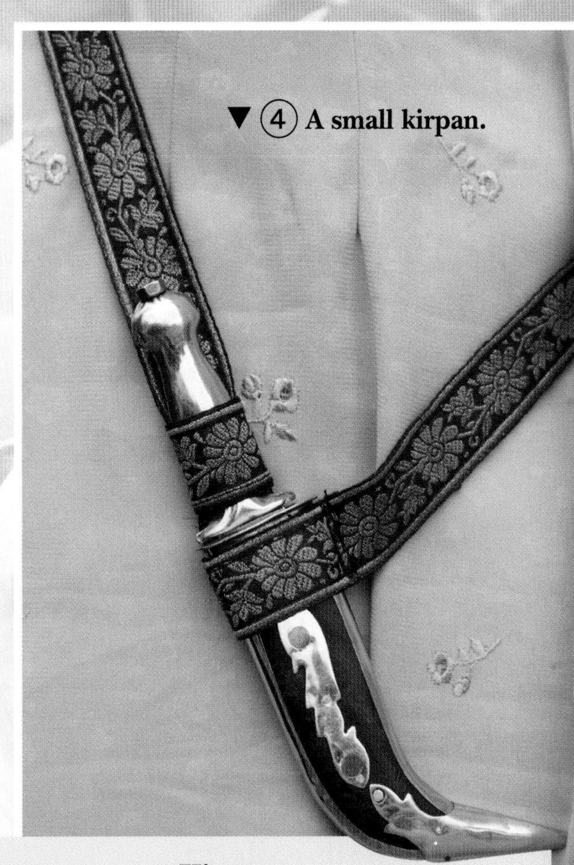

▼ ④ A small kirpan.

Kirpan

Many people in the Punjab used to carry swords to protect themselves and so Sikhs also began carrying swords, called kirpan, to protect themselves. Today, however, many places have laws against carrying things like swords, so many Sikhs wear smaller swords (picture ④), or even tiny swords around their necks instead (picture ③).

The sword is a reminder that Sikhs should always have courage and be ready to protect themselves and the weak.

▲ ⑤ Kaccha underwear.

Kaccha

When Sikhism began, many people in the Punjab wore only a loose cloth around their waists and did not wear any underwear. This made it hard to move freely and quickly. So, Sikhs began wearing a type of underwear called kaccha (picture ⑤) so that they could move easily and quickly without embarassment.

The kaccha helps Sikhs to remember that they should be ready to move quickly to defend themselves and to help others at all times. It is also a reminder to be modest.

What makes a gurdwara?

Many of the parts of the gurdwara are designed to remind people of some of the important lessons of Sikhism.

According to Sikh tradition, a gurdwara can be any building that has a roof and that contains a copy of the Guru Granth Sahib. However, most gurdwaras have at least two main parts (picture ④).

The first part of the gurdwara is the main hall, called the **DARBAR** or diwan hall (see pages 10–11). This is where worship takes place and where the Guru Granth Sahib is read out loud.

▶ ② The Sikh flag, the nishan sahib.

▲ ① Many gurdwaras have domes, as a reminder of how important Punjabi buildings looked when Sikhism began.

The second part of the gurdwara is a room where people go to share a meal after worship. This room is called the **LANGAR** (see pages 16–17).

There is also a smaller room where the Guru Granth Sahib is kept at night. This smaller room is called the **SACHKAND**.This is the holiest room in the gurdwara and is usually also the highest room in the gurdwara, perhaps on the top floor.

Symbol of the gurdwara

On the outside of the gurdwara there is always a yellow or orange triangular flag, called the nishan sahib (picture ②). The flag tells people that the building is a gurdwara. On the flag you can see the symbol of Sikhism, called the **KHANDA** (picture ③).

Doors and domes

A gurdwara usually has doors or windows on all four sides of the building. This is a reminder that the gurdwara is open to anyone.

▶ (3) The khanda is made up of three parts. In the centre of the symbol is a double edged sword, which stands for separating truth from lies. The circle around the sword stands for the fact that God has no beginning or end, like a circle. The two curved swords stand for the fact that a Sikh has obligations to both God and to society.

Many gurdwaras are built with a dome to remind Sikhs of the building style that was common in the Punjab when Sikhism began (pictures (1) and (2)). At that time, many important buildings were built with domes.

There is always a light on in the gurdwara, to show that God's light is always present, and that anyone is welcome to the gurdwara at any time.

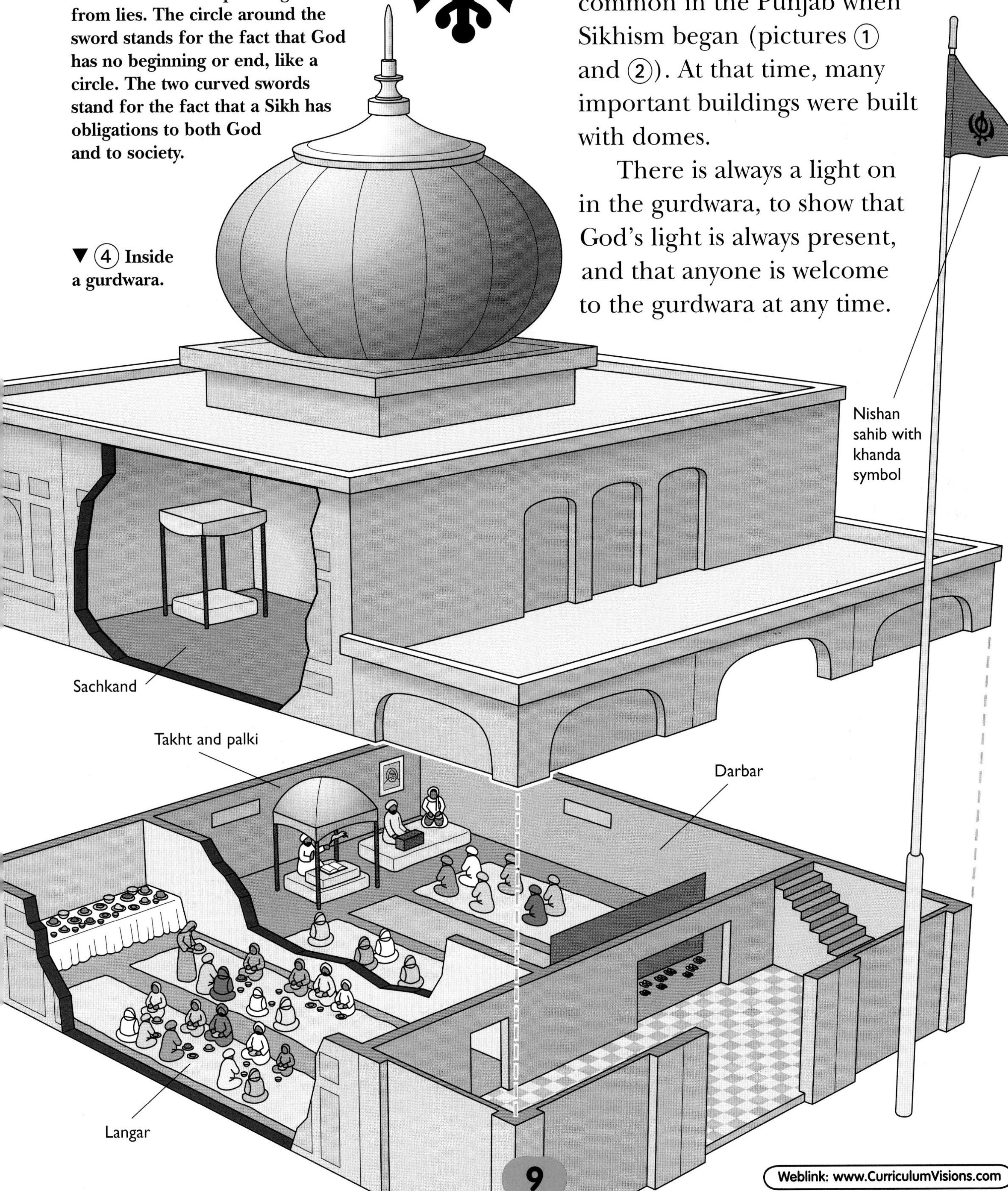

▼ (4) Inside a gurdwara.

Nishan sahib with khanda symbol

Sachkand

Takht and palki

Darbar

Langar

What the darbar is used for

The darbar is where the Sikh holy book is seen and read from during worship.

The main use of the darbar is for worship services, which always focus on the Sikh holy book, the **GURU GRANTH SAHIB**.

A throne for the Guru

Whenever it is in the darbar the Guru Granth Sahib is placed on a raised platform, called a **TAKHT**, which means throne (picture ①). The platform is covered by a canopy, called a **PALKI,** and has cushions where the Guru Granth Sahib is placed. The takht is usually placed along one wall of the darbar, so that all the worshippers can see it.

▲ ① This picture shows a takht in a large gurdwara. The Guru Granth Sahib is underneath the turquoise cloth, which protects it when it is not being read. The metal box in front of the takht is for people to leave offerings of money in. The money is used to help run the gurdwara. You can also see carrier bags containing food offerings that will be used in the langar.

▶ ② These musicians are playing traditional Punjabi instruments during worship.

In front of the takht there is a place for worshippers to leave offerings of money or food. These are used to help support the day to day costs of the gurdwara.

Sikh worship usually involves singing, accompanied by music so on one side of the takht is a place for the musicians, or **RAGIS**, to sit and play their instruments (picture ②).

Inside the darbar

There are no chairs in the darbar. Everyone sits on the floor during worship (picture ③). This way, no one is higher than the Guru Granth Sahib and everyone is equal.

▼ ③ There are no chairs in the darbar, so that no one is higher than the Guru Granth Sahib. Everyone worships sitting down.

To make sitting more comfortable, there is usually carpet on the floor of the darbar.

Art in the darbar

Sikhs believe that God does not have any form or shape. So there are no pictures of God in the darbar. There are also no candles, incense, bells or other objects, because Sikhs do not believe in using these things in worship.

But there may be some kind of artwork in the gurdwara and the darbar. One common kind of art in the gurdwara are paintings or murals of the ten Sikh gurus or of important events in the history of Sikhism. But in many gurdwaras, there may be just a large painting or even stained glass window, showing the "Ik onkar" or "khanda" (see picture ③ page 5).

The Guru Granth Sahib

The Guru Granth Sahib is the most important thing in the gurdwara.

The **GURU GRANTH SAHIB** is more than just a book, it is also the religious leader, or guru, of Sikhism (pictures ① and ③). So Sikhs treat the Guru Granth Sahib in many of the same ways that they would treat a human guru.

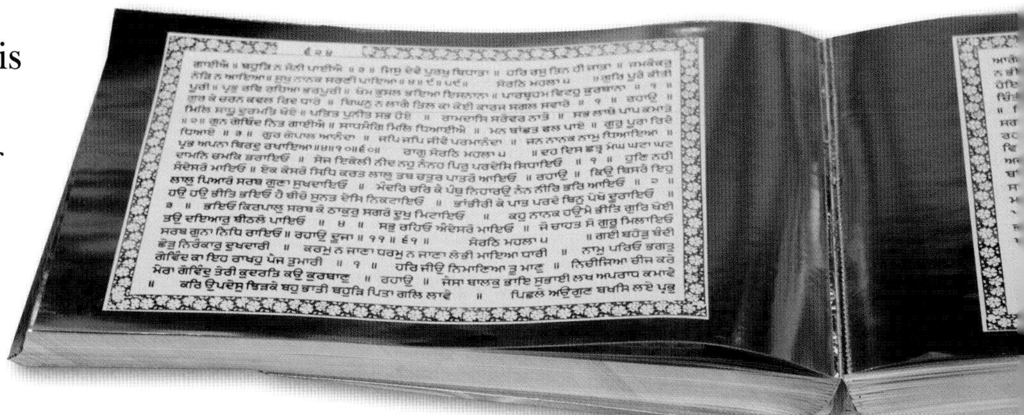

▲ ① The Guru Granth Sahib.

For example, if a person is having a problem they might ask the Guru Granth Sahib for advice by opening the book at random, reading the first verse they see, and then thinking about how the message of that verse can help them.

Or, when a baby is born, the parents might ask the Guru Granth Sahib to help them name the baby by opening the book at random, and using the first letter of the first verse on the left hand page as the first letter of their baby's name.

▼ ② The granthi is waving a chauri over the covered Guru Granth Sahib.

Handling the holy book

The Guru Granth Sahib is put away each night in a room of its own, called the **SACHKAND**. In the morning, before dawn, the book is taken back to the darbar.

During worship, the person who reads from the Guru Granth Sahib holds a fan of animal hairs, called a **CHAURI**, which they wave over the book as they read (picture ②). This reminds worshippers of how rulers and kings in ancient Punjab were treated.

Showing respect

Sikhs do not worship the Guru Granth Sahib, but many of the things Sikhs do in the gurdwara are done in order to show respect to the Guru Granth Sahib and to its teachings. For example, when Sikhs enter the darbar, they kneel in front of the Guru Granth Sahib.

When sitting in the darbar, everyone is very careful not to turn their back or to point their feet at the Guru Granth Sahib. This is because, in Punjabi culture, pointing your feet at someone is considered very rude.

Sikh priests

Worship services may be led by any adult Sikh, but are often led by a priest, called a **GRANTHI**.

▼ ③ The Guru Granth Sahib uncovered on the takht.

Anyone can be a granthi, including women. The granthi must be able to read Punjabi, and should be very learned in the Sikh religion and history.

The granthi also takes care of the Guru Granth Sahib, puts it away in the sachkand at night, and carries it into the darbar in the morning. Granthis also perform marriages and may give the sermons during services.

Worshipping in the darbar

Worship services take place in the darbar.

▼▶ ① When worshippers enter the darbar, the first thing they do is bow in front of the Guru Granth Sahib. Then they sit down and begin to worship.

◀ ② These children are singing hymns during worship.

In the gurdwara, group worship, called **DIWAN**, can take place at any time and on any day. In the UK, the most popular day for group worship is Sunday, as that is the day when most people are not at work.

In a large gurdwara, worship might continue for many hours, or even for an entire day, with people entering and leaving all the time (picture ①).

▼ ③ **Worshippers leave offerings of food or money to the gurdwara.**

As they enter the darbar, each person bows to the Guru Granth Sahib (picture ①) and leaves an offering (picture ③), then greets the congregation in a low, quiet voice with the words "*Waheguru ii ka Khalsa, sri Waheguru ji ki fateh*", which mean "The Sikh owes allegiance to God, sovereignty belongs to God alone".

Worship services

Music is a very important part of Sikh worship, and singing hymns, called **KIRTAN**, is a large part of every worship service (picture ②).

Services begin with the singing of a hymn, called Asa Di Var, written by Guru Nanak. Other hymns from the Guru Granth Sahib are then sung, accompanied by musical instruments.

Next, a part of the Guru Granth Sahib is read out loud and a sermon or talk which discusses the reading is given. This is followed by the singing of a hymn called Anand Sahib, written by Guru Amar Das, the third guru.

The congregation then stands with their eyes closed facing the Guru Granth Sahib for a prayer called **ARDAS**. During the prayer the word "Waheguru" (Punjabi for "praise to the guru") is often said, and this has much the same role as the word "amen" in Christian services.

Ceremonial food

At the end of the service, everyone is given a food called **KARDH PARSHAD**, which is a sweet made from flour, sugar and butter (picture ④).

◀ ④ **Sikhs believe that when they share the sweet kardh parshad, they are also sharing the blessings of God.**

What the langar is used for

The langar is a place for sharing food and being part of a community.

Every large gurdwara has a separate room or building called a **LANGAR** (pictures ① and ②). The langar is a community kitchen, where meals are prepared and eaten by anyone who comes to the gurdwara. The langar is a very important part of the gurdwara. It is both a charity and a part of worship.

A type of charity

In many large gurdwaras, the langar is a way to help the poor. Everyone is welcome to come and eat for free in the langar – they do not have to be a Sikh. Some large gurdwaras might feed hundreds or even thousands of needy people every day.

In the langar, the people who cook and serve the food are all volunteers. Volunteering is also called **SEWA**, or service (picture ③).

◀▼ ① Eating in the langar is a part of worship for Sikhs. Everyone eats together in a line, so that no one is higher or lower than anyone else.

When people come to worship at the gurdwara, they often bring donations of food, which are used in the langar. Every Sikh is expected to contribute what they can to the langar, either by giving food or money, or by helping to cook, serve and clean.

A type of worship

For Sikhs, eating at the langar is also a type of worship. After worship services, Sikhs go to the langar and eat a meal together. This is called the **PANGAT**. Sikhs believe that sharing food helps people to understand each other better, creates a feeling of friendship and equality and helps to build a stronger community.

▼ ② On holidays, the langar may move outside into the street, where food and drink are given free to anyone who passes by.

◄▲ ③ All the food in the langar is cooked by volunteers. A large gurdwara may feed thousands of people every day, so huge pots and many volunteers are needed. Sikhs believe that cooking and serving the poor and other worshippers helps them to be humble and to think about God.

Everyone is equal

Whenever people eat at the langar, they all sit in a row, with people of different races, religions and economic status all sitting and eating together. This helps to remind people that everyone is equal.

Any kind of food can be cooked at the langar, but it must be vegetarian. Sikhs do not have to be vegetarian, but everyone is welcome in the langar, and because some people do not eat meat, only food that everyone can eat is served.

Special days at the gurdwara

Some Sikh festivals are celebrated inside the gurdwara, and some are celebrated in the neighbourhood around the gurdwara.

Many festivals celebrating important days in Sikh history are celebrated at the gurdwara.

Some festivals are celebrated with a ceremony called **AKHAND PATH**. This is a non-stop recitation of the entire Guru Granth Sahib. This takes 48 hours and is done by many people, who each take turns reading. The reading finishes on the day of the festival.

▼ (2) The granthi waves his chauri over the Guru Granth Sahib and ragi (musicians) play, just as they do inside the gurdwara.

▼ (1) A nagar kirtan is a ceremony where the Guru Granth Sahib is paraded around the neighbourhood of the gurdwara, led by five Sikhs carrying swords or Sikh flags. The nagar kirtan shown here was held to celebrate the 400th anniversary of the first Guru Granth Sahib being placed inside the Harimandir Sahib (The Golden Temple) in Amritsar, India (pages 22–23).

After the reading, there is hymn singing, music, lectures and talks.

An akhand path may also be done on other occasions, such as to celebrate a wedding or at the birth of a child.

▼▶ ③ **The nagar kirtan procession is led by Sikhs dressed in traditional clothing and carrying Sikh flags and swords.**

Festivals for the gurus

Many of the festivals celebrated at the gurdwara have to do with events in the lives of the ten Sikh gurus. These days are called **GURUPURABS**. Some important gurupurabs are: the birthday of Guru Nanak, the birthday of Guru Gobind Singh (the last guru), the day the first Guru Granth Sahib was placed in a gurdwara. Gurupurabs often involve an akhand path, but there may also be a ceremony called a nagar kirtan (pictures ①, ② and ③).

Gurupurab festivals also include singing hymns and giving out food and drink (langar) to the general public (see picture ② on page 17).

New Year

On April 13th there is celebration of the Sikh New Year with a festival called Baisakh. This festival also celebrates the day in 1699 that Guru Gobind Singh created the ceremony of **BAPTISM,** called Amrit sanskar.

In the Amrit ceremony, a person becomes a fully-fledged member of the Sikh community, called the **KHALSA**, and is responsible for following the principles and traditions of Sikhism, such as wearing the five Ks, treating all people as equal and not smoking tobacco or drinking alcohol.

Most Sikhs are baptised in the Amrit ceremony when they are about 14 years old. Often, Amrit ceremonies are held on gurupurabs or other festival days.

Visiting a gurdwara

At the gurdwara you will have a chance to meet Sikhs and learn more about Sikhism.

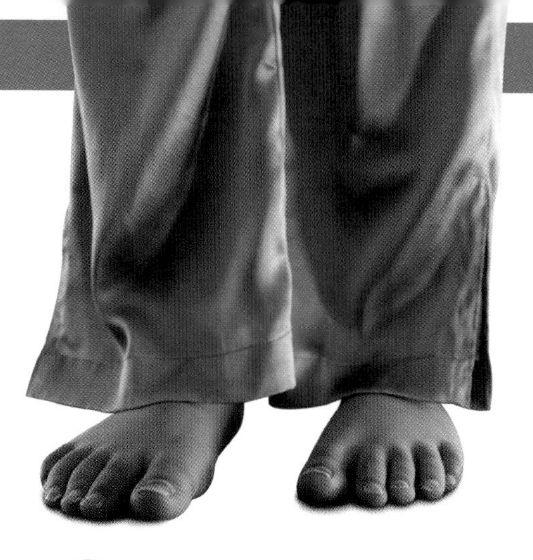

▲ (2) Everyone must take their shoes off in the gurdwara. You can wear socks or go barefoot.

You do not have to be a Sikh to visit a gurdwara. If you are not a Sikh, you will not be asked to worship or pray, but everyone who visits a gurdwara is expected to show respect.

Entering the gurdwara

Before you enter the gurdwara you can look for the flagpole and the flag. You can also look for any words written in Punjabi on the outside of the gurdwara (picture (1)). Are there four doors or windows to the building, or any domes on the roof?

When you enter the gurdwara, you will be asked to take your shoes off (picture (2)), and may also be asked to wash your feet. Except for young children, visitors are also expected to cover their heads. This can be with a scarf or other head covering (picture (3)).

You may see works of art on the walls that show scenes from Sikh history or symbols of Sikhism. Be sure to ask the person showing you around to explain what is in the artwork and how it was made.

◀▼ (1) Look for Punjabi writing on the outside of the building. The writing below says "gurdwara". As well as flags with the khanda symbol you may see the symbol used in other ways as in this posy of flowers above the door of a gurdwara.

What will we see and do in the darbar?

When you visit a gurdwara it will be daytime and the Guru Granth Sahib will be in the darbar. There may even be worship services going on, so you should make sure you are quiet and show respect.

When you sit down in the darbar, you will have to sit on the floor like everyone else – remember not to point your feet at the Guru Granth Sahib, because this is considered rude.

Only people who have washed and said special prayers can touch the Guru Granth Sahib, but you should notice the different ways that people show respect for the book and its teachings.

▲▼ (3) Everyone must cover their head inside the gurdwara. This Sikh boy is wearing a covering that usually goes under a turban and keeps the hair neat, but any kind of cloth covering can be worn. Girls and women can wear any kind of scarf.

Sharing a meal

You may also be taken for a meal in the langar (picture (4)). This is offered free to everyone who comes to the gurdwara, and you do not have to worship in order to eat in the langar. The point of sharing the meal is to remember that everyone is equal, so it doesn't matter who you sit next to.

▼ (4) Food served in the langar will all be vegetarian, so everyone can eat it.

The Golden Temple

The most important gurdwara is in India. It is The Golden Temple at Amritsar.

▲ ① The Golden Temple sits in a lake and is part of a large group, or complex, of buildings. This complex is surrounded by a wall with 18 gates and a white marble corridor.

In any part of the world where there are Sikhs, you can usually find a gurdwara. But some gurdwaras have special meaning for Sikhs.

The most important gurdwara in the world is the Harimandir Sahib, in Amritsar, India (picture ①). Harimandir Sahib means Temple of God. It is also called The Golden Temple or Darbar Sahib (Divine Court).

The Golden Temple is very large and beautifully decorated. It is covered in copper sheets and in gold leaf. But it also has all of the features that you have learned about in your studies of the Sikh gurdwara. For example, The Golden Temple has domes on the roof, doors on all four sides of the building, Sikh flags and khanda symbols.

You may also see some unique features. For example, The Golden Temple is the only gurdwara that is built in a lake. Guru Nanak, the founder of Sikhism, often came to this lake to think about God. Later, Sikh gurus enlarged the lake and built the gurdwara in the middle.

Unlike most other gurdwaras, The Golden Temple also has many shrines which remember important events. These are located on the walkway surrounding the outside of the gurdwara.

One shrine, the Dukh Bhanjani Ber marks the spot where it is said that a crippled child was healed after bathing in the lake. Another shrine, the shrine of Baba Deep Singh, marks the spot where a famous Sikh warrior died while fighting to protect other Sikhs. Along the outside of the gurdwara there are also plaques commemorating Sikhs who died in wars.

The large white buildings that surround the lake and the gurdwara contain langars and dormatories for the thousands of Sikhs and other visitors who come to the complex each day. Just like at a neighbourhood gurdwara, anyone can eat in the langar, and all the food is cooked and served by volunteers.

▼ (3) The annual raising of the nishan sahib (Sikh flag) at the Akal Takht (the sachkand for The Golden Temple) within The Golden Temple complex.

▼ (2) Sikhs line up to enter The Golden Temple and worship. Worship continues from before dawn until long after dark without stopping.

Index

Atlantic Europe Publishing

Teacher's Guide
There is a Teacher's Guide to accompany this book, available only from the publisher.

Dedicated Web Site
There's more about other great Curriculum Visions packs and a wealth of supporting information available at our dedicated web site:

www.CurriculumVisions.com

First published in 2003 by
Atlantic Europe Publishing Company Ltd

First reprint 2005. Second reprint 2006.

Author
Lisa Magloff, MA

Religious Adviser
Sri Guru Singh Sabha Gurdwara, Southall, London

Art Director
Duncan McCrae, BSc

Senior Designer
Adele Humphries, BA

Special photography
Graham Jepson

Acknowledgements
The publishers would like to thank the following for their help and advice:
Sri Guru Singh Sabha Gurdwara, Southall, London.

Photographs
The Earthscape Picture Library, except pages 22–23: photos courtesy *Hardeep Singh Sahota.*

Illustrations
David Woodroffe

Designed and produced by
Earthscape Editions

Printed in China by
WKT Company Ltd

Sikh gurdwara – *Curriculum Visions*
A CIP record for this book is available from the British Library
ISBN-10: 1 86214 446 X
ISBN-13: 978 1 86214 446 0

This product is manufactured from sustainable managed forests. For every tree cut down at least one more is planted.